Tranquillisers

The MIND Guide to Where to Get Help

Russell Murray
&
Donna Hurle
Department of Social & Economic Studies

Anthony Grant
Department of Modern Languages

First Published in 1991
MIND Publications
22 Harley Street, London W1N 2ED

© MIND (National Association for Mental Health) & University of
Bradford

Cover design and illustration by Judy Groves
Text designed by Joanne Crowther

ISBN 0-900557-91-5

for

John Viner Waterlow Cooper

1942 - 1988

Contents

Introduction

This directory is for people who want help to stop taking benzodiazepines (minor tranquillisers prescribed for anxiety or sleeplessness). It lists organisations who are prepared to help people with withdrawal and with associated problems.

BENZODIAZEPINE WITHDRAWAL

Although their use has decreased, benzodiazepines are the most commonly prescribed drugs used to reduce anxiety or insomnia. The best medical advice is that they should not be prescribed for longer than four weeks, and then only when the anxiety or insomnia is severe or disabling or subjecting the patient to unacceptable distress. The withdrawal of treatment should be gradual.

The recommended procedure for the management of withdrawal in general practice involves a stepwise reduction programme, typically extending over six to twelve weeks (although this will vary according to the progress made by the individual patient). It may begin with a switch of prescription to diazepam.

About a third of chronic users experience withdrawal symptoms. These can include both psychological and physical symptoms. They can mimic the symptoms for which the drug was prescribed and may lead the doctor or patient to the wrong conclusion that the drug must be restored.

While many people will manage without any support, others need assistance in coping. This can come from their GP or another trained or experienced person. A variety of different therapies are in use; it is unlikely that any one therapy will prove suitable for all users.

For many people, the difficulties they experience after withdrawing may be due also to the persistence of the underlying problems which caused the original anxiety or insomnia. If people are not given help to cope with these stresses, relapse is not surprising. It is now clear that many users will require support well beyond the end of the drugs.

ALTERNATIVES TO BENZODIAZEPINES

For the organisations listed here, helping people to withdraw is usually only part of their task. They give equal priority to helping people to cope with their problems without using drugs. This usually involves teaching other ways of coping with anxiety or sleeplessness.

THE DIRECTORY

Although we have tried to be thorough, we are bound to have overlooked some services. We hope that any users of the Directory who know of misssing groups will let us know for the next edition, see slip at back.

We have organised the groups into four categories.

TRANQUILLISER: Groups which offer some service specifically for tranquilliser users, even if the primary focus of the group is in some other field. For example, many general mental health or drug addiction projects now run special tranquilliser withdrawal groups.

ADDICTION: Groups whose primary focus is drug or alcohol or substance abuse, but who have stated that they will provide help to tranquilliser users.

MENTAL HEALTH: Groups whose primary focus is mental health, but who have stated that they will provide help to tranquilliser users.

OTHER: Groups who do not fit into any of the above categories, but who have stated that they will provide help to tranquilliser users.

None of the groups in the last three categories provide any services specifically for tranquilliser users. However, their staff should be aware of the problems of tranquilliser use, and usually the help they give will be the same as that offered by more specialised services.

Regardless of their focus, most of the groups listed in the Directory will provide counselling and other support during the withdrawal process.

COMMUNITY MENTAL HEALTH CENTRES & COMMUNITY PSYCHIATRIC NURSING SERVICES

These are two likely sources of help in most areas. For reasons of space we have not been able to include individual centres and services here. Every District Health Authority is responsible for providing community psychiatric nurses and most have now set up mental health centres.

OTHER SOURCES OF HELP

You may find that there are no services listed in this Directory for your area. That does not necessarily mean that there are no services in your area; it may be that we have missed them. If you cannot find what you are looking for in the Directory, we suggest that you try one of the listed national bodies, or contact one or more of the following organisations in your local area.

Community Health Council
Family Health Services Authority
Social Services Department
District Health Authority

How To Use This Directory

The services in this directory are listed by county; those in London are listed by borough. There is a town index at the back.

Within each area, the services are listed under four standard headings: Tranquilliser; Addiction; Mental Health; Other. These are explained in the Introduction.

For each service, we give the name, address, telephone number, and when they may be contacted. (The latter is not necessarily the same as the times at which the help is provided.) In addition, we indicate the type of organisation, and any restrictions that apply to possible clients.

Type of Organisation

NHS: Services provided under the National Health Service.

PUB (Public): Services provided by local or central government departments.

VOL (Voluntary): Services provided by local or national voluntary agencies.

PTE (Private): Services provided by private organisations who charge fees.

RESTRICTIONS

These generally fall into four areas.

Referral: Most of the services listed here allow people to refer themselves. However, some will only accept clients who have been referred by their General Practitioner or other doctor, or by some other professional, such as a Social Worker. **Open referral** means that people can refer themselves, **or** be referred by a third party. If anything else is indicated, potetential clients **cannot** refer themselves, but must be referred by someone else.

Appointments: Many groups allow people to turn up at their offices without an appointment; some have "drop-in" sessions. However, most prefer new clients to make an appointment first. Some organisations will not see people without an appointment.

Geographical: Most of the services listed here are restricted to people living within a specified catchment area.

Age/Gender/Ethnicity: A few groups restrict their services to specific client groups e.g. only women, only elderly people, only ethnic minorities.

For lack of space, we have not been able to list the range of facilities provided by each organisation.

INDEX OF COUNTIES

NATIONAL ORGANISATIONS

If you cannot find a suitable service in your area, it may be that one of the following can help you.

TRANXCALL
P.O. Box 440
Harrow
London
081 427 2065

Small registration fee and charge for written advice.

CITA (Council for Involuntary Tranquilliser Addiction)
Cavendish House Brighton Road
Waterloo
Liverpool
051 525 2777

RELEASE
388 Old Street
London EC1
071 729 9904 (emergency helpline 071 603 8654)

Narcotics Anonymous
PO Box 246
c/o 47 Milman Street
London SW10
071 351 6794/6066

Affiliated self-help groups throughout the country.

NATIONAL ORGANISATIONS

MIND
22 Harley Street
London W1N 2ED
071 637 0741

The Information Unit at MIND are maintaining a computer database of services for people with tranquilliser problems that will be more up to date than this Directory.

ALTERNATIVE MEDICINE

Many practitioners of alternative or complementary medicine offer help to people trying to come off tranquillisers. (Also, many of the services listed in the Directory offer such therapies as part of their work.) For reasons of space, we have not been able to list all those who responded to our survey. However, the following national bodies can give you the address of your nearest practitioner.

The Society of Homeopaths
2 Artizan Road
Northampton
NN1 4HU

Council for Acupuncture
Panther House
38 Mount Pleasant
London WC1X 0AP

ENGLAND
Avon

TRANQUILLISER

Bath Tranquilliser (Benzodiazepines) Withdrawal Support Group
2 New King Street
Bath
Tel: 0225 480794/480515

Thurs 1400-1530
VOL Open referral

ADDICTION

Bristol Drugs Project
18 Guinea Street
Redcliffe
Bristol BS1 6SX
Tel: 0272 298047

Mon-Fri 1000-1800
NHS PUB Open referral

Alcohol and Drugs Advisory Centre
5 Baker Street
Weston-super-Mare BS23 3AA
Tel: 0934 415376

Mon-Fri 1000-1700
VOL Open referral

Western Counselling Services Ltd
14 Walliscote Road
Weston-super-Mare BS23 1UQ
Tel: 0934 415711

Mon-Fri 0900-1700, Sat 0900-1300
PTE Has residential facilities. Open referral

Bath Area Drugs Advisory Service
1/2 Bridewell Lane
Bath BA1 1
Tel: 0225 469479

Mon/Tues/Fri 1000-1630,
Thurs 1000-1930
VOL Open referral

OTHER

Womankind
76 Colston Street
Bristol BS1 5BB
Tel: 0272 252 507

Mon-Fri 1000-1300
VOL Open referral. Women only

Wellwomen Information
24 St Thomas Street
Redcliffe
Bristol BS1 6JJ
Tel: 0272 221925

Tues/Weds 1000-1230 Drop-in
VOL Open referral

Bedfordshire

TRANQUILLISER

Valium, Ativan, Librium
Dependency Advisory Services
(VALDAS)
8 Farm Green
Farley Hill
Luton LU1 5PL
Tel:0582 416413 and 415836

24 hours
VOL Open referral GP referral

ADDICTION

Health Link - Drugs Advisory
Service
55 St. Peter's Street
Bedford MK40 2PR
Tel: 0234 270123

Mon-Fri 1000-1600
NHS Open referral

Luton Drug Helpline
34 Clarendon Road
Luton LU2 7PQ
Tel: 0582 32200

Mon-Fri 0900-1700
PUB GP or family referral.
Bedfordshire area

Berkshire

TRANQUILLISER

Drug Services Unit
156 Oxford Road
Reading RG1 7TJ
Tel:0734 391452

Mon-Fri Telephone 0900-1700,
Drop-in 1300-1700
NHS Open referral. Reading area

Rehabilitation Group Ltd
Huntercombe Manor
Huntercombe Lane South
Taplow
Maidenhead SL6 0PQ
Tel: 0628 667881
Mon-Fri 0900-1800
PTE Open referral

ADDICTION

East Berkshire District Drugs Team
District Department of Clinical
Psychology
Oak House
Upton Hospital
Slough SL1 2BJ
Tel: 0753 821789

Mon-Fri 0900-1700
NHS Open referral. East Berkshire
Health District

MENTAL HEALTH

Wokingham & District MIND
Station House
Station Approach
Wokingham
Tel: 0734 792620

Mon 1300-1600, Fri 1100-1500
VOL Open referral

OTHER

No. 22 - Windsor and Maidenhead Youth Counselling Service
22 Cookham Road
Maidenhead SL6 8AJ
Tel: 0628 36661

Mon/Wed 1200-1400 Mon-Thurs
1930-2130
VOL Open referral

Well Woman Association for West Berkshire
29 Queens Road
Reading
Tel: 0734 503157

Alternate Weds 1000-1300
every Thurs 1830-2130
VOL Open referral

Buckinghamshire

TRANQUILLISER

Counselling on Drug and Alcohol Centre
3 Priory Avenue
High Wycombe
Tel: 0494 461361

Mon-Fri 0930-1700
NHS PUB Open referral

ADDICTION

Pegasus Alcohol and Drug Advisory Service
Cripps Lodge
Broadlands
Netherfield
Milton Keynes MK6 4JJ
Tel: 0908 668603

Mon-Fri 0930-1800
NHS Open referral; appointment
needed. Milton Keynes area

Bucks Council on Alcohol and Drugs
Bierton Road
Aylesbury HP20 1EU
Tel: 0296 25329

Mon-Fri 0900-1700
NHS PUB Open referral

Cambridgeshire

TRANQUILLISER

Tranquilliser Dependency Service
The Mill House
Brookfields Hospital
Mill Road
Cambridge
Tel: 0223 245926 ext. 2146

Mon-Fri 0900-1700
NHS Open referral. Cambridge area

DIAL (Drugs Information and Advice Line)
Petersfield
St Peter's Road
Huntingdon PE18 7DG
Tel:0480 413800

Mon-Fri 0900-1600
Tues/Thurs 0900-1730
NHS VOL Open referral

ADDICTION

Bridgegate
32 North Street
Peterborough
Tel: 0733 314551

Mon 1000-1300, Mon/Tues/Weds/
Fri 1400-1700, Thurs 1530-1930
PUB Open referral

Cheshire

Thomas Percival Clinic
Winwick Hospital
Warrington
Tel: 0925 55221 ext. 3465

Mon-Fri 0900-1700
NHS Open referral. Warrington,
Widnes, Runcorn, Mersey area

Barnabas Drug Centre
118a Mill Street
Macclesfield SK11 6NR
Tel: 0625 422100

Mon-Thurs 0900-1700
Fri 0900-1630
NHS PUB Open referral.
Macclesfield district

Community Drugs Team
46 Chesterway
Northwich CW9 5JA
Tel: 0606 47179/40535

Mon-Fri 0900-1630
NHS Open referral

Drug Dependency Clinic
74 Victoria Road
Widnes WA8 7RE
Tel: 051 423 5247

Mon-Fri 0900-1700
NHS Open referral

Turning Point
27 Hoole Road
Chester CH2 3NH
Tel: 0244 325875

Mon-Fri 1000-1700
VOL Open referral; appointments
only

Drug Dependency Clinic
9 Wilson Patten Street
Warrington WA1 1PG
Tel: 0925 415176

Mon-Fri 0900-1700
NHS GP referral

Mersey Regional Alcohol and
Drug Dependence Unit
Countess of Chester Hospital
Liverpool Road
Chester CH2 1BQ
Tel: 0244 364095/364088

Mon-Sun 0730-2100, 24 hour
Helpline
NHS Open referral

Cheshire

Halton Drug Dependency Clinic
74 Victoria Road
Widnes WA8 7RA
Tel: 051 423 5247

Mon-Fri 0800-1800
NHS Open referral

Lifeline Project
45 Wilson Patten Street
Warrington WA1 1PG
Tel: 0925 53261

Tues-Sat 0900-1600
VOL Open referral. Warrington area

Vale Royal Drugs Advice Centre
Bridge House
15 London Road
Northwich CW5 9EY
Tel: 0606 46212

Mon-Fri 0930-1600
VOL Open referral

OTHER

Self Help Resource Centre
Room 209
Birley Centre
Chichester Road
Hulme M15 5FU
Tel: 061 226 5225

Mon-Thurs 0930-1730
PUB Open referral. Manchester only

Cleveland

TRANQUILLISER

Tranx Group
Newlands Community Mental
Health Centre
41 Kirkleatham Street
Redcar TS10 1QH
Tel: 0642 490881

Mon-Fri 0930-1630
NHS PUB Open referral; Redcar,
Marske, & New Marske only

ADDICTION

**South Tees Health Authority
Drugs Advice and Counselling
Service**
63 Kings Road
North Ormesby
Middlesbrough TS3 6EP
Tel: 0642 242550

Mon-Fri 0900-1700
NHS Open referral
South Tees Health District

**Hartlepool Drugs Advisory
Service**
10 Grange Road
Hartlepool TS26 8JA
Tel: 0429 863046

0900-1700
VOL Open referral

Health Advice Centre
29/31 Yarm Lane
Stockton on Tees
Tel: 0642 607313

Mon-Fri 0930-1700
NHS VOL Open referral
appointment needed

MENTAL HEALTH

Toc H Friendship Circles
Webb House
7 Zetland Road
Middlesbrough TS1 1EH
Tel: 0642 230984

Mon-Fri 1000-1600
VOL Open referral, preferably with
consent of GP

Redcar MIND
First Floor
1 Milbank Terrace
Redcar TS10 1EE

Mon-Fri 0845-1500, Drop-in Mon/
Tues/Thurs/Fri 1100-1500,
Tues 1900-2100
VOL Open referral

Cornwall

ADDICTION

The Freshfield Service
10 Strangways Terrace
Truro TR1 2NY
Tel: 0872 41952

Mon-Fri 0900-1700
VOL Open referral

MENTAL HEALTH

Gwaynter Psychiatric Unit
City Hospital
Truro
Tel: 0872 74242

Mon-Fri 0900-1700
NHS Professional referral. Carrick
only

OTHER

Penzance Natural Health Centre
53 Morrab Road
Penzance TR18 4EX
Tel: 0736 60522

Mon-Fri 0900-1700
PTE Open referral

Cumbria

TRANQUILLISER

Drug and Alcohol Service
Workington Infirmary
Workington CA14 2UN
Tel: 0900-68739

Mon-Fri 0900-1700
NHS PUB Open referral

ADDICTION

Croft House Drugs and Alcohol Advisory Centre
96 Wigton Road
Carlisle CA2 3EP
Tel: 0228 49605

Mon/Fri 0900-2100, Tues-Thurs
0900-1700
NHS PUB Open referral

East Cumbria Health Authority Dependency Service
Croft House
96 Wigton Road
Carlisle CA2 3EP
Tel: 0228 49605

Mon/Fri 0900-2100
Tues-Thurs 0900-1700
NHS PUB Open referral

East Cumbria Health Authority Dependency Service
Cumberland House
Garlands Hospital
Carlisle
Tel: 0228 31081 ext. 2843

Residential, day programme 7 days
0700-2200
NHS Professional referral

MENTAL HEALTH

Ulverston MIND
Room 206, Coniston House
New Market Street
Ulverston
Tel: 0229-581578

Drop-in Mon 1000-1400
Tues 1400-1600, 1900-2100
Thurs 1000-1300
VOL Open referral

Derbyshire

TRANQUILLISER

Tranx-Release Derbyshire
81 Peveril Drive
Ilkeston DE7 8EA
Tel: 0602 304287

Mostly 24 hour
VOL Open referral

ADDICTION

Turning Point - Derby Drugline
(Tranxline)
2nd Floor
Willow House
Willow Row
Derby DE1 3NZ
Tel: 0332 292166

Mon-Fri 1000-1600
Thurs 1000-1800
VOL Open referral; appointment
preferred. South Derbyshire only

MENTAL HEALTH

Derby Counselling and Therapy
Centre
125 London Road
Derby DE3 8FP
Tel: 0332 366863

Mon-Fri 1000-2100
VOL Open referral. Appointment
required

Devon

TRANQUILLISER

TASHA (Tranquilliser Addiction Self Help Association)
Lynn Piper
4 Smithfields
Totnes TQ9 5LR
Tel: 0803 867249

Daily 1700-2200
VOL Open referral; appointment needed

Plymouth and District MIND
Beaumont Hall
19 North Street
Saint Judes
Plymouth PL4 8PS
Tel: 0752 268631

Mon-Fri 1000-1600
VOL Open referral

ADDICTION

The Quay Centre
Rolle Quay House
Rolle Quay
Barnstaple EX31 1JE
Tel: 0271 44454

Mon/Fri 1300-1600, Tues/Thurs 1000-1600, Weds 1000-1300
NHS VOL Open referral; appointment preferred

Broadreach House
465 Tavistock Road
Plymouth PL6 7HE
Tel:0752 790000

24 hrs
VOL Open referral; appointment needed. Fees charged to those who can afford them

Drugs and Alcohol Resource Team
17 Howell Road
Exeter EX4 4LG
Tel: 0392 214570

Mon-Thurs 0900-1700, Fri 0900-1630
NHS PUB GP/Professional referral; appointment needed

Torbay District Addictions Service
39 Abbey Road
Torquay TQ2 5NQ
Tel: 0803 291129

Mon-Fri 0900-1700
NHS PUB Advice giving only for benzodiazepine users

Devon

MENTAL HEALTH

Victory Centre
Dean Clarke House
Southernhay East
Exeter
Tel: 0392 211321

Mon-Thurs 0900-1700, Fri 0900-1300
PUB Open referral

OTHER

Plymouth Nuffield Clinic
Lipson Road
Plymouth PL4 8NQ
Tel:0752 660281

Mon-Fri 0900-1700
NHS Open referral

Dorset

ADDICTION

East Dorset Drugs and Alcohol Advisory Service
Bungalow 6
Royal Victoria Hospital
Gloucester Road
Boscombe
Bournemouth BH7 6JF
Tel: 0202 304455

Mon-Fri 0900-1700
VOL Open referral

Durham

TRANQUILLISER

North East Council on Addictions (Durham)
Shakespeare Hall
North Road
Durham DH1 4SQ
Tel: 091 383 0331

Mon-Fri 0900-1700
PUB VOL Open referral

Community Addictions Advisory Service
Health Centre
Dalton Way
Newton Aycliffe DL5 4PD
Tel: 0325 300427

Mon-Fri 0830-1630
NHS PUB Open referral. South
West Durham Health Authority area

Easington District Alcohol and Drug Advisory Centre
2nd Floor, 30 Yoden Way
Peterlee SR8 6HN
Tel: 091 587 2194

Mon-Fri 0900-1700
NHS PUB Withdrawal advice only
with GP's assent

Mrs. H. M. Hogarth
27 Cradock Street
Bishop Auckland DL14 6HB
Tel: 0388 602012

Mon-Sun 1000-2100
PTE Open referral

Tackle It
Parish Centre
Church Chare
Chester-le-Street

Thurs 1300-1500
VOL Open referral

ADDICTION

District Drug and Alcohol Advice Service
Health Promotion Unit
Maiden Law Hospital
Lanchester DH7 0QN
Tel: 0207 503456 ext. 737

Mon-Fri 0900-1600
NHS Open referral. North West
Durham Health District

Durham

Addiction Prevention Service
Addiction Centre
Archer Street
Darlington DL3 6LT
Tel: 0325 483703

Mon-Fri 0900-1600
NHS Open referral

MENTAL HEALTH

Darlington MIND
33 Duke Street
Darlington DL3 7RX
Tel: 0325 283169

Mon-Fri 0930-1600
VOL Open referral. Darlington area

Calm Contact
Thomas Street
Consett DH8 5PB
Tel: 0207 501051

Mon-Thurs 1200-2000
PTE (small charge) Open referral

Essex

TRANQUILLISER

Community Drug Advice Service
Elm Park Clinic
252 Abbs Cross Lane
Hornchurch RM12 4YG
Tel: 04024 52402

Mon-Fri 0930-1700
NHS Open referral; telephone first.
Barking, Havering and Brentwood

Community Drug Advice Service
Oxlow Lane Clinic
Oxlow Lane
Dagenham RM10 7YU
Tel: 081 592 7748

Mon-Fri 0930-1700
NHS PUB Open referral; telephone
first. Barking, Havering and
Brentwood

Martello Court Tranquilliser Withdrawal & Support Group
Martello Court
Clacton & District Hospital
Freeland Road
Clacton
Tel: 0255 421145 ext. 340

Tues 1115-1230
NHS Open referral; appointment
needed. Clacton area

Tranquilliser Advice Service
Sunnyside Centre
Orsett High Road
Orsett
Grays
Tel: 0375 891100 ext. 2665

Tues 1700-2200, Thurs 1400-1900
NHS PUB Open referral;
appointment needed

Billericay Tranquilliser Support Group
c/o The Health Centre
Stock Road
Billericay
Tel: 0268 583500

Thurs 1000-1200
VOL Open referral. Basildon and
Thurrock area

Colchester MIND (Tranquilliser Support Group)
Winsley's House
High Street
Colchester
Tel: 0206 760362

Alternate Mondays 1900-2100
VOL Open referral

Essex

The Beacon Trust, Vange Community Centre
Vange Hill Drive
Vange, Basildon
Tel: 0268 583500

Mon-Fri 0900-1700
VOL Open referral. Basildon and
Thurrock area

Redbridge Community Drug and Alcohol Service
Gate Cottages
Chadwell Heath Hospital
Romford RM6 4XJ
Tel: 081 599 3007 ext. 5263

Mon-Fri 0900-1730, Mon/Wed/
Thurs 1830-2000, Drop-in Mon/
Thurs 0900-1700, 24 hour Helpline
081 503 8718
NHS PUB Open referral;
appointment needed

ADDICTION

Southend Drug Advisory and Treatment Service
District Office
Rochford Hospital
Union Lane
Rochford
Tel: 0702 541516

Mon/Thurs/Fri 0845-1600, Tues/
Weds 0845-1700
NHS Open referral; appointment
preferred

North East Essex Drug Advisory Service
1 Hospital Road
Colchester CO3 3HQ
Tel: 0206 48481

Mon-Fri 0930-1700
NHS Open referral; appointment
needed. North East Essex area

Drugline Essex
Madeira Grove Clinic
Woodford
Tel: 081 599 2260

Drop-in Tues/Weds 1930-2200
NHS Open referral

Drugline Essex
Church House
Market Place
Romford
Tel: 0708 749151

Drop-in Mon 1930-2200
VOL Open referral

Drugline Essex
Helpline Southend on Sea
Tel: 0702 74391

Drugline Essex
Helpline Chelmsford
Tel: 0245 414653

Essex *continued*

Community Drug Team
New Writtle Street Centre
New Writtle Street
Chelmsford CM2 0RW
Tel: 0245 351441

Mon-Fri 0900-1700
NHS Open referral

Alcohol and Drugs Advisory Service (West Essex)
David Livingstone Centre
St. Michael's Close
Harlow CM20 3QH
Tel: 0279 641347

Mon-Fri 0930-1730, Tues 0930-
2000; Helpline 0279 438716
VOL appointment needed

MENTAL HEALTH

Abberton Day Hospital, The Lakes
Colchester General Hospital
Turner Road
Colchester CO4 5JL
Tel: 0206 853535 ext. 2804

Mon-Fri 0900-1700
NHS GP referral. Colchester area

Gloucestershire

TRANQUILLISER

Gloucestershire MIND
80 Westgate Street
Gloucester
Tel: 0452 416575

Mon-Fri 0900-1500
VOL Open referral. Gloucester area

ADDICTION

Gloucestershire Drugs Project
24 Cambray Place
Cheltenham GL50 1JN
Tel: 0242 570003

Mon-Fri 0900-1700
PUB VOL

Cheltenham/Gloucester Community Drug Team
Coney Hill Hospital
West Lodge Drive
Coney Hill GL4 7QJ
Tel: 0452 617033 ext. 2337/8

Mon-Fri 0900-1700
NHS PUB Open referral

Cheltenham Community Drugs Team
Delancey Hospital
Charlton Lane
Cheltenham
Tel: 0242 527784

Mon-Fri 0900-1700
NHS GP referral; Cheltenham area

MENTAL HEALTH

Gloucestershire Institute for Personal Development
P.O. Box 6
Coleford GL16 7EX
Tel: 0594 60016

Mon-Fri 0900-1700
PTE Open referral; appointment needed

Denmark Road Day Hospital
18 Denmark Road
Gloucester
Tel: 0452 25061

Mon-Fri 0900-1700
NHS GP referral

GREATER LONDON

Barnet

ADDICTION

Drug Concern (Barnet)
Woodlands
Colindale Hospital
Colindale Avenue NW9 5HG
Tel: 081200 9575/905 9955

Mon-Tues 0930-1945, Weds-Fri 0930-1730
NHS Open referral; telephone first

Camden

TRANQUILLISER

MIND in Camden
Barnes House
9-15 Camden Road NW1 9LQ
Tel: 071 911 0815

Mon 1400-1700, Tues-Thurs 1030-1700
VOL Open referral; telephone first.
Camden area

Brent

ADDICTION

Brent Community Drug Service
Block G
Central Middlesex Hospital
Acton Lane
Tel: 081 965 9716

Mon-Fri 0900-1700
NHS Open referral. Brent only

GREATER LONDON

Ealing

TRANQUILLISER

Ealing Drugs Advisory Service
14 Alexandria Road W13
Tel: 071 579 5585/6

Mon-Fri 1000-1700
NHS VOL Open referral. Preference
to Ealing residents

ADDICTION

**Regional Alcoholism and Drug
Dependence Unit**
St. Bernards Hospital
Southall UB1 3EU
Tel: 081 574 2444 ext. 2419

Mon-Fri 0900-1700
NHS Open referral

MENTAL HEALTH

**Avenue House Community
Mental Health Resource Centre**
43/47 Avenue Road
Acton W3
Tel: 081 993 7781

Mon-Fri 0900-1700
NHS Open referral. London W3 area

Enfield

ADDICTION

Grovelands Priory Hospital
The Bourne
Southgate N14 6RA
Tel: 081 882 8191

24 hours
PTE Open referral

Enfield Community Drug Team
2a Forest Road
Edmonton N9 8RX
Tel: 081 443 3272

Mon-Thurs 0900-1700
Fri 0900-1600
NHS PUB Open referral

GREATER LONDON

Greenwich

ADDICTION

The Beresford Project
8 Beresford Square
Woolwich SE18 6BB
Tel: 081 854 9518

Mon-Fri 0930-1630
NHS PUB Open referral

MENTAL HEALTH

St. John's Centre for Mental Health
68 The Heights
Charlton SE7
Tel: 081 858 9516

Mon-Sun 1000-2200
PUB Open referral. Greenwich area

Hackney

TRANQUILLISER

City and Hackney MIND
8-10 Tudor Road E9 7SN
Tel: 081 533 6565

Mon-Fri 1000-1700
VOL Open referral

ADDICTION

Hackney Drug Dependency Unit
Hackney Hospital
Homerton High Street E9 6BE
Tel: 081 986 6816

Mon-Fri 0900-1700
NHS Open referral. Hackney area

OTHER

Asian Women's Support Group
31b Chatsworth Road E5
Tel: 081 986 4804

Mon-Fri 1000-1500
VOL Open referral. Asian women Hackney area

GREATER LONDON

Hammersmith & Fulham

TRANQUILLISER

Benzodiazepine Clinic
Charing Cross Hospital
Fulham Palace Road W6 8RF
Tel: 081 846 1511

Mon-Fri 0930-1700
NHS Open referral

ADDICTION

Accept Services
724 Fulham Road SW6 5SE
Tel: 071 371 7477/7555

Mon-Fri 0900-1700
NHS Open referral; telephone first

MENTAL HEALTH

White City Mental Health Project
c/o Hammersmith and Fulham
Social Services
129 Bloemfontein Road W12 7DA
Tel: 081 749 9451

Mon-Fri 1000-1700
PUB Open referral. Women only

Women's Action for Mental Health
131 Bloemfontein Road
White City Estate
Shepherd's Bush W12
Tel: 081 749 9446

Mon-Fri 1030-1530
VOL Open referral. Women on White City estate only

Hammersmith & Fulham MIND
153 Hammersmith Road
W14 0QL
Tel: 081 741 0661

Mon-Fri 1000-1730
VOL Open referral

GREATER LONDON

Haringey

ADDICTION

Drugs Advisory Service Haringey (DASH)
St. Ann's Centre for Health Care
St. Ann's Road
Tottenham N15 3TH
Tel: 081 802 0443

Mon-Fri 0900-1700
NHS Open referral. Appointment
only. Haringey area

MENTAL HEALTH

**Women and Medical Practice
40 Turnpike Lane N8 0PS
Tel: 081 888 2782**

Mon-Fri 1000-1700
PUB VOL Open referral;
appointment needed

Harrow

TRANQUILLISER

Tranxcall
P.O. Box 440
Tel: 081 427 2065

Mon-Fri 0900-1700
PTE Open referral. Small
registration and charge for written
advice

Hillingdon

ADDICTION

Hillingdon Community Drug Team
Fountains Mill
81 High Street UB8 1JR
Tel: 0895 250414/5

Mon-Fri 0900-1700
NHS PUB Open referral

GREATER LONDON

Hounslow

ADDICTION

Tranquilliser Anxiety Self-Help Association
78 St. John's Road
Isleworth TW7 6RU
Tel: 081 862 6724 and 569 9933

Mon-Fri 1000-1800
NHS Open referral; appointment needed

Ethnic Counselling Network
170a Heston Road
Tel: 081 577 6059

Mon-Fri 1000-1700
PUB Open referral. Ethnic minorities only

MENTAL HEALTH

The Berkeley Centre
27 Cranford Lane
Heston TW5 9EP
Tel: 081 570 5200

Mon-Fri 0900-1700
PUB PTE Open referral; appointment needed

Islington

ADDICTION

The Angel Drug Project
38-44 Liverpool Road N1 OPU
Tel: 071 226 3113

Mon/Weds/Fri 1400-1700 Drop-in and 1400-2000 Tues/Thurs
VOL Open referral

MENTAL HEALTH

NAFSIYAT -The Intercultural Therapy Centre
278 Seven Sisters Road N4 2HY
Tel: 071 263 4130

Mon-Fri 1000-1700
VOL PUB Self referral, GP referral preferred. Ethnic and cultural minority people. Non-Islingtonians pay

GREATER LONDON

Kensington

ADDICTION

Promis Recovery Centre
2a Pelham Street SW7
Tel: 071 584 6511

Mon-Fri 0900-1900
PTE Free telephone advice between
0900-1900

Promis Recovery Centre
1 Saint Quintin Avenue W10
Tel: 081 969 0917

Mon-Fri 0900-1700
PTE Free telephone advice between
0900-1700

Charter Clinic Chelsea
1-5 Radnor Walk SW3 4PB
Tel: 071 251 1272

Mon-Fri 0900-1700
PTE Open referral

Lambeth

ADDICTION

Substance Misuse Unit
St. Thomas Hospital
Lambeth Palace Road SE1 7EH
Tel: 071 633 0720

Mon-Fri 1400-1700
NHS Professional referral. Lambeth
area

MENTAL HEALTH

Waterloo Community
Counselling Project
Barleymow Clinic
Tanswell Estate
Frazier Street SE1
Tel: 071 928 3462

Tues 1830-2030, Thurs 0945-1545
VOL Open referral. Lambeth and
Southwark

Lambeth MIND
245a Coldharbour Lane SW9
Tel: 071 737 6884

Telephone and Drop-in Mon-Fri
1400-1700
VOL Open referral

GREATER LONDON

Lewisham

TRANQUILLISER

Community Team for Mental Health in the Elderly
Hither Green Hospital
Hither Green Lane SE13
Tel: 081 698 4611 ext. 8158

Mon-Fri 0900-1700
NHS Open referral; appointment needed. Clients over 65

MENTAL HEALTH

Kirkdale Resource Centre
200 Kirkdale
Sydenham SE26 4NL
Tel: 081 676 0441

Mon-Fri 1000-1600
NHS PUB GP/Professional referral

Newham

MENTAL HEALTH

Newham District Psychology Service
30 Edith Road E6 1DE
Tel: 081 472 4661 ext. 5091

Mon-Fri 0900-1700
NHS GP referral preferred. Newham only

East Ham Centre
Shrewsbury Road E7 8QR
Tel: 081 472 4661

Mon-Fri 0900-1700
NHS GP referral. Newham area

GREATER LONDON

Southwark

TRANQUILLISER

Chaucer Day Hospital
Lower Road
Rotherhithe SE16
Tel: 071 231 4578

Mon-Fri 0900-1700
NHS Open referral. SE1, SE16,
SE17 only

ADDICTION

The Blackfriars Road Clinic
St. Georges Clinic
151 Blackfriars Road SE1 8EL
Tel: 071 620 0192

Mon 1400-1900, Weds 1000-1700,
Fri 1000-1230
NHS Professional referral,
appointment needed

GREATER LONDON

Tower Hamlets

TRANQUILLISER

East London Drug Project
Oxford House
Derbyshire Street E2
Tel: 071 729 8008

Mon-Fri 1800-2000
VOL Open referral

ADDICTION

Release
388 Old Street
Tel: 071 729 9904

Mon-Fri 1000-1800; emergency
helpline number 071 603 8654)
VOL Open referral

Drug Dependency Unit
St. Clements Hospital
2a Bow Road E3 4LL
Tel: 071 377 7975

Mon-Fri 0900-1700; Drop-in Mon-
Thurs 1600-1700
NHS Open referral; appointment
needed (except for Drop-in)

OTHER

London Black Womens Health
Action Project
Cornwall Avenue
Bethnel Green E2
Tel: 081 980 3503

Mon-Fri 0900-1700
PUB Open referral

GREATER LONDON

Waltham Forest

ADDICTION

ACCEPT Waltham Forest
1 Beulah Road E17
Tel: 081 509 1888

Mon-Fri 1000-1700
NHS VOL Open referral;
apppointment needed

Wandsworth

ADDICTION

Galsworthy Lodge
The Priory Hospital
Priory Lane
Roehampton SW15 5JJ
Tel: 081 392 1238

Mon-Fri 0900-1800
PTE Open referral

Addiction Treatment Clinic
Queen Mary's University
Hospital
Roehampton Lane SW15 5PN
Tel: 081 789 6611 ext 2309

Mon 1100-1900
Tues-Fri 0900-1700
NHS Open referral

Drug Dependency Unit
St. George's Hospital
Blackshaw Road
Tooting SW17
Tel: 081 672 9881

Mon-Fri 0900-1700, 24 hour
Helpline 081 767 8711
NHS Open referral; appointment
needed. Tooting area

GREATER LONDON

Westminster

TRANQUILLISER

Charter Nightingale Hospital
11-19 Lisson Grove NW1 6SH
Tel: 071 258 3828

24 hours
PTE Open referral

ADDICTION

Westminster Drug Project
470 Harrow Road
Maida Vale W9 3RU
Tel: 071 286 3339

Mon-Fri 0900-1800
PUB VOL Open referral;
appointment needed

Richmond Fellowship
10 St. Stephen's Crescent W2
5QT
Tel: 071 229 3710

24 hours
VOL Open referral

Drug and Alcohol Foundation
38 Ebury Street SW1W 0LU
Tel: 071 730 6796

Mon-Fri 0900-1700
VOL Open referral; appointment
needed

Greater Manchester

TRANQUILLISER

Tranxact
129 Wellington Road South
Stockport SK1 3TS
Tel: 061 477 7196

Thurs 1900-2100
VOL Open referral. Stockport area

Tranquilliser Self-Help Group
Salford Women's Centre
89 Rowan Close
Churchill Way
Salford M6 5AL
Tel: 061 736 3844

Mon-Fri 0930-1530
VOL Self-referral; Drop-in centre
Manchester area

Support Group (StressRelief)
Baguley Health Centre
Hall Lane
Manchester M23
Tel: 061 998 5711

Mon-Fri 0900-1700
Drop-in Fri 1330-1500
NHS VOL Open referral

ADDICTION

Bolton Community Drug Team
27 Mawdsley Street
Bolton BL1 1LN
Tel: 0204 397129

Mon-Thurs 0930-1630
NHS Open referral. Bolton area

Bury Community Drug Team
5a Silver Street
Bury BL9 0EU
Tel: 061 797 6068

Mon-Fri 0900-1700
NHS PUB Open referral

Wigan and Leigh Community Drug Team
14 Brown Street North
Leigh WN7 1BU
Tel: 0942 608618

Mon-Fri 0900-1230/1330-1630
NHS Open referral

Tameside & Glossop Community Drugs Team
133 Astley Street
Dukinfield SK16 4PU
Tel: 061 344 5365

Mon-Fri 0900-1700
NHS Open referral. Tameside &
Glossop

Greater Manchester

South Manchester Community Drug Team
Sharston Community Centre
Fenside Road
Wythenshawe
Manchester
Tel: 061 428 7848

Mon-Fri 0900-1700
NHS VOL Open referral

Lifeline Manchester
101-103 Oldham Street
Manchester M4 1LW
Tel: 061 839 2054

Mon-Fri 0930-1700
VOL Open referral

Central Manchester Community Drugs Team
Acorn House
4 Denmark Road
Manchester M15 6FG
Tel: 061 274 4287

Mon-Fri 0900-1630
NHS PUB Open referral

Salford Community Drug Advisory Service
173 Fountain Square
Chorley New Road
Swinton
Manchester M27 2AE
Tel: 061 793 0907

Mon-Fri 0900-1630
NHS PUB Open referral. Salford area

North Manchester Community Drugs Team
Cheetham Probation Office
20 Humphrey Street
Cheetham Hill
Manchester M8 7JR
Tel: 061 721 4394

Mon-Fri 0930-1630
NHS PUB VOL Open referral.
North Manchester Health District

Stockport Community Drug Team
129 Wellington Road South
Stockport SK1 3TS
Tel: 061 476 2533

Mon-Fri 0900-1700
NHS PUB Open referral;
appointment needed. Stockport area

MENTAL HEALTH

Clinical Psychology Department
Birch Hill Hospital
Rochdale
Tel: 0706 77777

Mon-Fri 0900-1700
NHS GP referral. Rochdale area

Greater Manchester continued

St. Georges Day Centre
United Reformed Church
St. Georges Road
Bolton
Tel: 0204 381179

Mon 0900-1530
Telephone Mon-Fri 0900-1700
NHS PUB Open referral;
appointment necessary

Stockport and District MIND
Churchgate House
96 Churchgate
Stockport SK1 1YJ
Tel: 061 480 7393

Mon-Thurs 0930-1730
Fri 0930-1700
VOL Open referral. Stockport area

Brindle House
34a Church Street
Hyde SK14 1JJ
Tel: 061 366 8040/0313

Mon-Thurs 0900-1700, Fri 0900-
1600
NHS PUB Open referral. Hyde and
Glossop area

Hampshire

TRANQUILLISER

Community Drugs Advisory Service
St. Paul's Hospital
St. Paul's Hill
Winchester SO22 5AA
Tel: 0962 840900

Mon-Fri 0930-1700
NHS Open referral

ADDICTION

Portsmouth Drugs Advice Centre
Northern Road
Cosham PO6 3EP
Tel:0705 324636

Mon-Fri 0900-1700
NHS Open referral. Hampshire region

Basingstoke Drug Advice Centre
The Flat
Hackwood Road Hospital
Hackwood Road
Basingstoke RG21 3AB
Tel: 0256 469006

Mon-Fri 1400-1700
NHS Open referral

Interface
Town Hall Centre
Leigh Road
Eastleigh SO4 4DE
Tel: 0703 620260

Mon-Thurs 1000-16000
NHS PUB Open referral;
appointment preferred. Eastleigh area

Northern Road Clinic
Northern Road
Cosham
Tel: 0705 324636

Mon-Fri 0900-1200, 1400-1630
NHS Open referral. Cosham area

Hampshire *continued*

MENTAL HEALTH

District Psychology Service
Adult Mental Health Section
Connaught House
63B Romsey Road
Winchester
Tel: 0962 825139

Mon-Fri 0900-1700
NHS Professional referral.
Winchester area

Marchwood Priory Hospital
Hythe Road
Marchwood
Southampton SO4 4WU
Tel: 0703 840044

Mon-Fri 24 hours
PTE Open referral

Hereford & Worcester

TRANQUILLISER

C.O.T. (Coming Off Tranquillisers)
The Edward Parry Centre
Radford Avenue
Kidderminster
Tel: 0562 743436 and 746010

Mon-Thurs 0900-1700
Fri 0900-1600
VOL Open referral

ADDICTION

Herefordshire Community Drug Service
27a St. Owen Street
Hereford HR1 2JB
Tel: 0432 263636

Mon-Fri 0930-1630
NHS Open referral. Hereford region

Hereford and Worcester Alcohol Advisory Service
10 Sansome Place
Worcester
Tel: 0905 27417

Mon-Fri 0900-1700
NHS PUB Open referral. Hereford and Worcester area. Only deals with benzodiazepine problems in connection with alcohol abuse

Hereford and Worcester Alcohol Advisory Service
21 Kings Street
Hereford HR4 9BX
Tel: 0432 357825

Mon-Weds 0900-1700
NHS PUB Open referral. Hereford and Worcester area. Only deals with benzodiazepine problems in connection with alcohol abuse

Hereford and Worcester Alcohol Advisory Service
165a Birmingham Road
Bromsgrove
Tel: 0527 78585

Weds/Thurs 0930-1600
NHS PUB Open referral. Hereford and Worcester area. Only deals with benzodiazepine problems in connection with alcohol abuse

Substance Misuse Service
Worcester Royal Infirmary
Newtown Road
Worcester
Tel: 0905 763333 ext. 33249

Mon-Fri 0830-1700
NHS PUB Open referral

(continued)

Bromsgrove & Redditch
Community Drug Team
165a Birmingham Road
Bromsgrove
Tel: 0527 31593

Mon-Fri 0900-1700
NHS PUB Open referral

MENTAL HEALTH

Kidderminster General Hospital
Department of Psychology
Bewdley Road
Kidderminster DY11 6RJ
Tel: 0562 823424 ext. 3296

Mon-Fri 0900-1700
NHS GP referral. Kidderminster
area

Malvern MIND
c/o 9 North End Lane
Malvern WR14 2ET
Tel: 0684 574709

Wed 1015-1200, Sun 1430-1630
VOL Open referral; appointment
preferred

Hertfordshire

TRANQUILLISER

TRANX-CARE
c/o Drugcare
29 Upper Lattimore Road
St. Albans AL1 3UA
Tel: 0727 34539

Mon-Fri 0900-1700, Drop-in 1000-1200/1330-1530
24 hour helpline 0727 34539
VOL Open referral

ADDICTION

Stevenage and North Hertfordshire Drugsline
The Voluntary Centre
Swingate
Stevenage SG1 1RU
Tel: 0438 364067

Mon-Fri 0930-1230 and 1400-1700
NHS PUB VOL Open referral

Stevenage and North Hertfordshire Drugsline
Thomas Bellamy House
Bedford Road
Hitchin SG5 1HL
Tel: 0462 442442

Mon-Fri 0930-1200 and 1400-1700
NHS PUB VOL Open referral

Hertfordshire and Bedfordshire Standing Conference on Drugs Abuse
Room 1, Top Floor
Danesbury Hospital
Welwyn
Tel: 043 871 6847

Mon-Fri 0900-1700
VOL Open referral

MENTAL HEALTH

Stevenage MIND
Danestrete Centre
Southgate
Stevenage SG1 1HB
Tel: 0438 815437

Mon 1000-1200, 1930-2130; Thurs 1930-2130
VOL Open referral

Watford & District MIND
16 Anthony Close
Watford WD1 4NA
Tel: 0923 34862

Drop-in Sat 1300-1700,
Telephone Mon-Sun 0900-2200
VOL Open referral

Humberside

TRANQUILLISER

Hull and East Yorkshire Council for Drug Problems
6 Wright Street
Hull HU2 8HU
Tel: 0482 225868

Mon-Fri 0930-1700, Tranx line
0482 229871
VOL Open referral

ADDICTION

IMPACT
23-25 Battery Street
Immingham DN40 1AZ
Tel: 0469 571345

Tues/Fri 1000-1700
NHS PUB Open referral

IMPACT
18 Brighowgate
Grimsby DN32 0QX
Tel: 0472 251351

Mon-Fri 100-1700
NHS PUB Open referral

MENTAL HEALTH

Scunthorpe & District MIND
'Printers Yard'
Fenton Street
Scunthorpe DN15 6QX
Tel: 0724 871497

Mon-Fri 0900-1700
VOL Open referral; telephone first

Grimsby/Cleethorpes & District MIND
50 Oole Road
Cleethorpes
Tel: 0472 602502

Mon/Wed/Fri 1000-1600, Drop-in
Thurs 1400-1600, 1900-2100
VOL Open referral

North Humberside MIND
30 Percy Street
Hull HU2 8HL
Tel: 0482 224729

Mon-Fri 1000-1600
VOL Open referral

Isle of Wight

MENTAL HEALTH

The Cedars Day Unit
18 Queens Road
Ryde PO33 3BG
Tel: 0983 67426

Mon-Fri 0900-1600
NHS GP or Consultant referral

Isle of Wight Youth Trust
1 St. Johns Place
Newport
Tel: 0983 529569

Mon-Fri 0900-1700
VOL Open referral
Under 25 years only

Kent

ADDICTION

'38' Drug Advice Centre
38 West Cliff Road
Ramsgate CT11 9NT
Tel: 0843 596638

Mon-Fri 0900-1300, 1400-1700
PUB Open referral. Canterbury and
Thanet area

Drug Link
The Hollies
Stone House Hospital
Cotton Lane
Dartford DA2 6AU
Tel: 0322 293728

Mon-Fri 0900-1700
NHS Open referral. Dartford area

The Addiction Treatment Centre
4 Manor Road
Chatham ME4 6AG
Tel: 0634 830114

Mon-Fri 0900-1700
NHS PUB Open referral; Medway
area

Promis Recovery Centre
Old Court House
Pinners Hill
Nonington CT15 4LL
Tel: 0304 841700

Mon-Fri 0900-1700
PTE Free telephone advice between
0900-1700

Inside Out, Drug Advice Centre
St. George's
7 Chilston Road
Tunbridge Wells TN4 9LP
Tel: 0892 34422

Mon-Fri 0930-1730
NHS PUB Open referral. Tunbridge
Wells area

Milestones Community Drug Team
East Lodge
1 Old Bexley Lane
Bexley DA5 2BW
Tel: 0322 559058

Mon-Fri 0900-1700
NHS PUB Open referral;
appointment needed. Bexley only

Cornerstone
49/50 Marsham Street
Maidstone
Tel: 0622 690944

Mon-Fri 0900-1700
NHS Open referral

Kent

MENTAL HEALTH

Department of Psychiatry
Ashford Hospital
London Road
Ashford
Tel: 0784 251188

Mon-Fri 0900-1700
NHS GP referral. Ashford area

Northover Mental Health Resource Centre
102 Northover
Downham
Bromley
Tel: 081 461 5577

Mon/Tues/Thurs/Fri 0930-1230
NHS PUB Open referral

MIND in Bexley
c/o The Crayford Centre
4/6 London Road
Crayford
Tel: 0322 521646

Drop-in Weds/Thurs 1400-1600,
Telephone Mon-Fri 1000-1230
VOL Open referral

OTHER

The Wealden Clinic
48 Grosvenor Road
Tunbridge Wells TN1 2AS
Tel: 0892 545443

Mon-Fri 0900-1700
PTE Open referral; appointment
needed

Blackthorn Trust
475 Tonbridge Road
Maidstone ME16 9LH
Tel: 0622 726277

Mon-Fri 0900-1700
VOL Open referral, with GP's
approval. Kent area

Lancashire

Preston Community Drug Team
St. Thomas Institute
Appleby Street
Preston PR1 1HX
Tel: 0772 204110

Mon-Fri 0830-1700
NHS Open referral. Preston area

Chorley and South Ribble MIND
'Open Mind Centre'
208 Stump Lane
Chorley PR6 0AT
Tel: 0257 260714

Mon-Fri 0930-2100, open weekends
VOL Open referral

Tameside and Glossop MIND
The MIND Centre
18 Chester Square
Ashton-Under-Lyne OL6 7NS
Tel: 061 330 9223 and 339 110

Mon-Thurs 0900-1700
VOL Open referral

West Lancashire Community Drug Team
75 Westgate
Skelmersdale WN8 8AZ
Tel: 0695 50740

Mon-Fri 0900-1700
NHS Open referral

Lancaster & District Community Drug Team
Ryelands House
Rylands Park
Lancaster LA1 2LN
Tel: 0524 663354/844309

Mon-Fri 0900-1700
NHS Open referral, Lancaster district

Blackburn Community Drug Team
The Penny Street Resource Centre
28 Penny Street
Blackburn BB1 6HL
Tel: 0254 680520

Mon-Fri 0900-1700
NHS Open referral

Drug Dependency Unit
The Health Centre
156 Whitegate Drive
Blackpool
Tel: 0253 63232 ext. 268

Mon-Fri 0900-1700
NHS Open referral; appointment needed. Lancashire only

Lancashire

Burnley, Pendle and Rossendale Community Drug Team
60 Westgate
Burnley BB11 1RY
Tel: 0282 32345

Mon-Thurs 0900-1300/1400-1630
Fri 0900-1300
NHS Open referral

NCH Drugline
2 Union Court
Union Street
Preston PR1 2HD
Tel: 0772 53840

Mon-Fri 0930-2130
Drugline 0772 825492
VOL Open referral; appointment advisable

Chorley and South Ribble Community Drug Team
14 West Lane
Chorley PR7 2SJ
Tel: 0257 230452

Mon-Fri 0900-1700
NHS Open referral. Chorley and Leyland area

OTHER

Preston Well Women Centre
2 Hardwick Street
Preston PR1 1TQ
Tel: 0772 555813

Mon-Fri 1000-1600
VOL Open referral. Women only

Leicestershire

TRANQUILLISER

Tranx-Leics
c/o 32 De'Montfort Street
Leicester LE1 7GD
Tel: 0533 555600

Mon-Fri 0900-1700 (Tel: 0533
692930 Mon-Sun 0800-2200)
VOL Open referral

ADDICTION

Leicestershire Community
Drugs Service
Paget House
2 West Street
Leicester LE1 6XP
Tel: 0533 470200

Every day 0900-2100 including
weekends and bank holidays
NHS PUB Open referral

Lincolnshire

TRANQUILLISER

Gainsborough MIND
The Neighbourhood Centre
North Parade
Gainsborough
Tel: 0427 810056

Weds 1400-1600
VOL Open referral

ADDICTION

Ferdowse Clinic
Heckington Manor
Heckington, Nr. Sleaford
Tel: 0529 61342/61343

Mon-Fri 1000-1700
PTE Open referral; appointment
needed

Alcohol and Drugs Counselling Service
Portland House
3 Portland Street
Lincoln LN5 7JZ
Tel: 0522 521908

Mon-Fri 0830-1630
NHS Open referral

MENTAL HEALTH

Eastfield Day Centre (Mental Health)
Eastfield House
Eastfield Road
Louth LN11 7AN
Tel: 0507 600800

Mon-Fri 0900-1700
PUB Open referral. Louth area

Mental Health Unit
Rauceby Hospital
Rauceby, Nr. Sleaford
NG34 8PP
Tel: 0529 8241

Mon-Fri 0900-1700
NHS Open referral

Merseyside

TRANQUILLISER

Community Occupational Therapy Department
Fazakerley Hospital
Liverpool
Tel: 051 525 5980 ext. 3828

Mon-Fri 0830-1630
NHS GP/Consultant referral

Supportive Help Against Drugs Organisation (SHADO) Ltd.
120 Stonebridge Lane
Croxteth
Liverpool L11 9AZ
Tel: 051 546 1141/6556

Mon-Fri 0900-1700
VOL Open referral. Liverpool area

Consumer Network St. Helens
Windle Pilkington House
St. Helens
Tel: 0744 56578

Mon 1930-2100
VOL Open referral

Wirral Tranxhelp
The Under 5's Centre
St. Paul's Road
Seacombe
Tel: 051 630 1845

Wed 1930-2200
VOL Open referral

Council for Involuntary Tranquilliser Addiction (CITA)
Cavendish House
Brighton Road
Waterloo
Liverpool L22 5NG
Tel: 051 525 2777

Mon-Fri 1000-1730
PUB Open referral

ADDICTION

Merseyside Drugs Council (North Sefton)
46 Hoghton Street
Southport PR9 0RQ
Tel: 0704 534759

Mon-Fri 0900-1700
NHS Open referral

Merseyside Drugs Council
27 Hope Street
Liverpool
Tel: 051 709 0074

Mon-Fri 0900-1700
Tues 0900-1900
NHS Open referral; appointment preferred

Merseyside

Knowsley Drug Advice and Information Unit
Family Welfare Centre
Cherryfield Drive
Kirkby
Tel: 051 546 7111

Mon-Fri 0900-1700
Weds 0900-1930
PUB Open referral

Mersey Drug Training and Information Service
27 Hope Street
Liverpool L1 9BQ
Tel: 051 709 3511

Mon-Fri 0930-1730
Open referral

Merseyside Drugs Council
48 Claughton Street
St. Helens WA10 1SN
Tel: 0744 30072

Mon-Fri 0900-1630
NHS Open referral

MENTAL HEALTH

Liverpool MIND
236 County Road
Walton
Liverpool L4
Tel: 051 523 2712

Mon-Fri 0930-1600
PUB VOL Open referral;
appointment preferred

Norfolk

ADDICTION

Community Alcohol and Drug Service (NORCAS)
52a Dene Side
Great Yarmouth NR30 2HL
Tel: 0493 857249

Mon-Fri 0900-1700
Tues 0900-1900
NHS Open referral; appointment needed

Bure Centre
West Norwich Hospital
Bowthorpe Road
Norwich NR2 3UD
Tel: 0603 667955

Mon-Fri 0900-1700
NHS Open referral by appointment

West Norfolk and Wisbech Community Alcohol and Drug Service
4 Avenue Road
Kings Lynn PE30 5NW
Tel: 0553 761623

Mon-Fri 0900-1630
NHS Open referral

MENTAL HEALTH

Broadland Mental Health Support Team
North Bungalow
Parkside Drive
Old Catton
Norwich NR6 7DP
Tel: 0603 424932

Mon-Wed, Fri 0830-1630
NHS PUB Professional referral, Self referral occasionally accepted; ongoing work needs assent of GP Norwich (north) and Broadland district

Copper Kettle Day Centre (MIND)
11 Lower Goat Lane
Norwich NR2 1EL
Tel: 0603 615967

Mon-Fri 0930-1630
VOL Open referral

Northamptonshire

TRANQUILLISER

Tranx Release
Council on Addiction
Spring House
51 Spring Gardens
Northampton NN1 1LX
Tel: 0604 250976

Mon-Thurs 0930-1630
Fri 0930-1600
PUB Open referral

Northumberland

TRANQUILLISER

Harbour Day Unit
Blyth Community Hospital
Thoroton Street
Blyth
Tel: 0670 364040

Mon-Fri 0830-1630
NHS Open referral; appointment
needed. Blyth area

ADDICTION

Northumberland Alcohol and Drug Project
75a Station Road
Ashington NE63 8RS
Tel: 0670 852322

Mon-Fri 1000-1600
NHS PUB Open referral;
appointment needed

MENTAL HEALTH

Ashmore House
Green Lane
Ashington NE63 0EY
Tel: 0670 855866

Mon-Fri 0900-1700
NHS PUB Open referral. Ashington
area

OTHER

Blyth Valley Well Woman Centre
22 Beaumont Street
Blyth NE24 1HP
Tel: 0670 368000

Mon 1400-1600, Thurs 1900-2100,
Fri 1000-1200
VOL Open referral. Women only

Women's Health Advice Centre
1 Council Road
Ashington NE63 8RZ
Tel: 0670 853977

Mon-Thurs 1030-1430, Tues 1830-2030
VOL Open referral; appointment
needed. Women only

Nottinghamshire

TRANQUILLISER

Bassetlaw MIND
6 Hardy Street
Worksop
Tel: 0909 476075

Mon-Fri 0900-1700
VOL Open referral

Escape
16 James William Turner Avenue
Sutton-in-Ashfield NG17 5BP
Tel: 0623 556590

Mon-Fri 0900-1700
VOL Open referral

Tranx Release
Beeston Volunteer Bureau
46a High Road
Beeston
Tel: 0602 225238

Mon-Fri 0930-1500
VOL Open referral

ADDICTION

Drug Dependents Anonymous (D.D.A.)
1 Newcastle Chambers
Off Angel Row
Nottingham NG1 6HQ
Tel: 0602 412888

Mon-Fri 1000-1700
VOL Open referral. Nottingham/
Trent region

Alcohol/Drug Unit
Mapperley Hospital
Porchester House
Castle Day Centre
Porchester Road
Nottingham NG3 6AA
Tel: 0602 691300

Mon-Fri 0930-1730
NHS Open referral. Lincolnshire/
South Derbyshire/Central
Nottinghamshire

MENTAL HEALTH

Nottingham Counselling Centre
32 Heathcoat Street
Nottingham
Tel: 0602 501743

Mon-Fri 0900-1700
VOL Open referral; apppointment
needed

Oxfordshire

TRANQUILLISER

ACORN/Oxford MIND
Cowley Community Centre
Barns Road
Cowley
Oxford
Tel: 0865 716633

Mon-Thurs 1000-1500
VOL Open referral

ADDICTION

Ley Community
Sandy Croft
Sandy Lane
Yarnton
Oxford OX5 1PB
Tel: 08675 71777

Mon-Fri 1000-1700
NHS Open referral

Oxford Community Drug and Alcohol Team
Ley Clinic
Littlemore Hospital
Littlemore OX4 4XN
Tel: 0865 223276

Mon-Fri 0900-1700
NHS Open referral

Oxfordshire Council on Alcohol and Drug Abuse
1 Tidmarsh lane
Oxford OX1 1NG
Tel: 0865 244447

Mon-Fri 1000-1700
VOL Open referral

MENTAL HEALTH

Psychology Department
Warneford Hospital
Oxford
Tel: 0865 226430

Mon-Fri 0830-1900
NHS Open referral, but GP informed

Shropshire

ADDICTION

Drug Help
3 Haygate Road
Wellington
Telford TF1 1QX
Tel: 0952 222229

Mon 1400-1700
Tues-Fri 1000-1700
NHS PUB Open referral; Shropshire
area

Somerset

TRANQUILLISER

Rosebank Mental Health Centre
Priory Park
Glastonbury Road
Wells BA5 1TH
Tel: 0749 73787

Mon-Fri 0900-1700
NHS Open referral. Wells area

Yeovil Withdrawal from Minor Tranquillisers Group
Penn House Day Hospital
Penn Hill
Yeovil
Tel: 0935 75377

Mon-Fri 0900-1700
NHS Open referral. Yeovil area

Frome Tranx Group
Community Mental Health
Centre
'Cairnsmoor'
Nunney Road
Badcox
Frome BA11 4LA
Tel: 0373 73905

Mon-Fri 0900-1700
NHS Open referral, but prefers GP
to be informed and involved

ADDICTION

DEAL
Portway
Wells BA5 2BG
Tel: 0749 77791

Mon-Fri 0900-1700
VOL Open referral

Somerset Council on Alcohol and Drugs
3 Upper High Street
Taunton TA1 3PX
Tel: 0823 288174

Mon-Fri 0900-1700
NHS PUB Open referral

Yeovil Drug Line
35 Higher Kingston
Yeovil BA21 4AS
Tel: 0935 32622

Mon-Fri 0900-1700
Drop-in 1000-1200
NHS Open referral

Staffordshire

Coton House Addiction Unit
St. George's Hospital
Corporation Street
Stafford
Tel: 0785 57888 ext. 5031

24 hours
NHS Professional referral

Substance Abuse Unit
City General Hospital
Newcastle Road
Stoke-on-Trent ST4 6QG
Tel: 0782 715444 ext. 2316

Mon-Fri 0900-1700
NHS Professional referral.
Appointment only. North
Staffordshire

Druglink-North Staffs
Hope Street Centre
76-82 Hope Street
Hanley
Stoke-on-Trent ST1 5BX
Tel: 0782 202139

Mon/Weds 1130-1630
Tues 0930-2100
Thurs/Fri 0930-1630
NHS PUB VOL Open referral
Stoke-on-Trent area

Tran-Ex
61 Foston Avenue
Burton-Upon-Trent DE13 0PL
Tel: 0283 63016

24 hour telephone service
VOL Open referral

Release Group
Greenhill Health Centre
Church Street
Lichfield
Tel: 0543 414311

Mon-Fri 0830-1630
NHS Open referral; appointment
needed. Lichfield area

ADDICTION

South East Staffordshire
Drugline Centre (Turning Point)
47a Station Street
Burton Upon Trent DE14 1AX
Tel: 0283 512255

Mon/Wed/Fri 1000-1600
NHS VOL Open referral
South East Staffordshire

Staffordshire *continued*

South East Staffordshire Drugline Centre (Turning Point)
Tamworth Drugline centre
12a Colehill
Tamworth B79 7HE
Tel: 0827 310660

Weds/Thurs 1000-1600
Fri 1000-1300
NHS VOL Open referral
South East Staffordshire

Turning Point Stafford Drugline & Advice on Addiction Centre
92 Wolverhampton Road
Stafford ST17 4AH
Tel: 0785 51820

Mon-Thurs 1000-1500
Fri 1200-1500
NHS VOL Open referral
Mid-Staffordshire

Mid-Staffs MIND
131/141 North Walls
Stafford ST16 3AD
Tel: 0785 53569

Mon-Thurs 0900-1300
VOL Open referral; appointments preferred

North Staffs MIND
44 Curch street
Stoke-on-Trent ST4 1BL
Tel: 0782 46363

Mon-Fri 0900-1700
VOL Open referral

MENTAL HEALTH

Friary Centre
St. Michael's Hospital
15a Trent Valley Road
Lichfield WS13 6EF
Tel: 0543 263424

Mon-Fri 0830-1700
NHS GP/Consultant referral.
Lichfield area

Suffolk

ADDICTION

Community Drug Team
40 Bond Street
Ipswich IP4 1JE
Tel: 0473 236069

Mon-Fri 0900-1700
NHS PUB Open referral
East Suffolk Health District

Waveney Alcohol & Drugs Service (WADS)
Alexandra Resource Centre
62-64 Alexandra Road
Lowestoft
Tel: 0502 587311 ext. 217

Mon-Fri 0900-1700
NHS PUB Open referral
appointment needed
Waveney district

Adfam (Suffolk)
P.O. 35
Woodbridge IP12 4NW
Tel: 0394 461443

Mon-Fri 0930-1200
VOL Open referral. Suffolk only

OTHER

Waveney Womens Health Information Centre
21 Milton Road East
Lowestoft NR 32 1NT
Tel: 0502 561816

Mon/Weds 1000-1300
Thurs 1000-1600/1830-2030
VOL Open referral. Women only

Surrey

Relaxation for Living
29 Burwood Park Road
Walton upon Thames KT12 5LH
Tel: 0932 227826

Mon-Fri 0900-1700
PTE Open referral

South West Surrey Drug and Alcohol Clinic
Buryfields House
Buryfields
Guildford GU2 5AZ
Tel: 0730 61662

Mon 1400-1700
Thurs 1400-1700/1800-2100
NHS Open referral; appointment
needed. S.W. Surrey residents

Drug Concern (Croydon) Ltd
76a Southbridge Road
Croydon CR0 1AE
Tel: 081 681 8113

Mon-Fri 0930-1730
VOL Open referral. Croydon only

Surrey Counselling Service
49 Russell Hill Road
Purley CR8 2XB
Tel: 081 668 7359

Mon-Fri 0900-1700
VOL Open referral; appointment
needed

Drug Problem Helpline
22a South Street
Epsom KT18 7PF
Tel: 0372 743434

24 hours
VOL Open referral

Drug Dependence Clinic
Brookwood Hospital
Knaphill
Tel: 04867 4545

Mon-Thurs 1000-1700
NHS GP referral

St. Joseph's Centre for Addiction
Holy Cross Hospital
Hindhead Road
Haslemere GU27 1NQ
Tel: 0428 656517

24 hours
PTE Open referral

Surrey

Community Substance Abuse Services
Frith Cottage
Church Road
Frimley GU16 5AD
Tel: 0276 62566

Mon-Fri 0830-1700
NHS PUB Open referral

Surrey Alcohol and Drug Advisory Service
21 Kingsway
Woking GU21 1NU
Tel: 0483 579313

Mon-Fri 0900-1700
PUB Open referral

Surrey Drug Care
Leapale Road
Guildford GU1 8JN
Tel: 0483 300112

24 hours
VOL Open referral

Abraham Cowley Unit
Holloway Hill
Lyne
Chertsey KT16 0AE
Tel: 0932 872010 ext. 3309

Mon-Fri 0900-1700
NHS Professional referral
Chertsey area

MENTAL HEALTH

Kenley Psychiatric Unit
Kingston Hospital
Galsworthy Road
Kingston-upon-Thames
Tel: 081 546 7711

Mon-Fri 0900-1700
NHS Open referral

Emmaus Centre
Abele Grove
2 Dorking Road
Epsom KT18 7LT
Tel: 03727 21155

Mon-Fri 0830-1800
Also Tues-Thurs 1800-2100
PTE Professional referral

Sussex (East)

ADDICTION

DAIS
38 West Street
Brighton BN1 2RE
Tel: 0273 21000

Mon-Fri 0900-1300/1400-1700
NHS Open referral

Libra Hastings
The Southwater Centre
Southwater Road
St. Leonards on Sea TN37 6LB
Tel: 0424 430134

Mon-Fri 0900-1700
VOL Open referral

LIBRA
Unit 4
Vincent's Yard
Susans Road
Eastbourne BN21 3YG
Tel: 0323 644629

24 hour telephone advice
on 0273 477100
VOL Open referral. Eastbourne area

Community Alcohol Team
82 Queens Road
Brighton
Tel: 0273 207304

Mon-Fri 0900-1700
NHS Open referral (preferably
informimg GP) appointment needed

The Libra Trust
1 & 2 Corporation Villas
North Street
Lewes BN7 2PJ
Tel: 0273 477100

Mon-Fri 0900-1700; advice and
information: 24 hour live helpline
PUB Open referral

The Seaside Centre Y.M.C.A.
95 Seaside Road
Eastbourne BN21 3PL
Tel: 0323 412412

Mon-Fri 1200-1600
VOL Open referral

MENTAL HEALTH

Colville Clinic
Grange Road
Eastbourne BN21 4HE
Tel: 0323 646231

Mon-Fri 0900-1700
PTE Professional referral
required

Burnt Mill Community Mental Health Centre
33 London Road
Uckfield
Tel: 0825 761177

Mon-Fri 0900-1700
NHS Open referral. Uckfield area

Sussex (East)

Avenida House
3 Upper Avenue
Eastbourne
Tel: 0323 22744 ext. 330

Mon-Fri 0900-1700
NHS Open referral; appointment
preferred

Self-Help for Stress
174 Surrenden Road
Brighton BN1 6NN
Tel: 0273 553557

Mon-Fri 0900-1700
VOL Open referral; appointment
needed

OTHER

Nestor Medical Services Ltd.
Ticehurst House Hospital
Ticehurst
Wadhurst TN5 7HU
Tel: 0580 200391

Open 24 hours
PTE

Sussex (West)

ADDICTION

The Summit
22 Sudley Road
Bognor Regis
Tel: 0243 869234

Drop-in Tues/Thurs 0930-1200
NHS Open referral

Crawley Association for the Prevention of Addiction
'The Tree' (Annexe)
103 High Street
Crawley
Tel: 0293 562856

Mon-Fri 1000-1500
Telephone 24 hours
PUB Open referral

Options
29 Wordsworth Road
Worthing BN11 3NJ
Tel: 0903 204539

Mon-Fri 0900-1700
NHS PUB Open referral

Substance Abuse Unit
Crawley Hospital
West Green Drive
Crawley RH11 7DH
Tel: 0293 551134

Mon-Fri 0900-1700
NHS Open referral

Tyne & Wear

TRANQUILLISER

North Tyneside Alcohol and Drug Problem Service
1 Cleveland Road
North Shields
Tel: 091 258 7047

Mon-Fri 1000-1600
NHS Open referral

North East Council on Addictions
Mid Tyne NECA Centre
Civic Hall
Ellison Street
Jarrow NE32 3HZ
Tel: 091 483 9999
Mon-Fri 0900-1600
VOL Open referral

Sunderland Alcohol and Drug Advice Centre
17 Vine Place
Sunderland SR1 3NA
Tel: 091 510 1999

Mon-Fri 0900-1700
VOL Open referral
Sunderland and Washington area

Tranquilliser Advice and Support Project
c/o North East Council on
Addictions (NECA)
1 Mosley Street
Newcastle-upon-Tyne NE1 1YE
Tel: 091 232 0797

Mon-Fri 0830-1630
PUB Open referral

ADDICTION

The Alcohol & Drug Problem Service
Plummer Court
Carliol Place
Newcastle upon Tyne NE1 6UR
Tel: 091 230 1300

Mon-Fri 0900-1700, 24 hour
counselling line 091 230 0203
NHS Open referral. North East
(Plus Cumbria, Teeside,
Northumberland)

Turning Point: Whitley Bay Substance Dependency Project
61 Marine Avenue
Whitley Bay NE26 1NB
Tel: 091 251 1725

Mon-Fri 0900-1700
VOL Open referral

Tyne & Wear *continued*

North East Council on Addictions (NECA)
Gateshead Centre
Swinburne House
12 Swinburne Street
Gateshead NE8 1AX
Tel: 091 490 1045

Mon-Fri 0830-1630
VOL Open referral

NECA (North East Council on Addictions)
6 Stanhope Road
South Shields NE33 4BU
Tel: 091 456 9999

Mon 0900-1200
Tues-Fri 0900-1300
NHS Open referral

Community Addiction Team
11 Norfolk Street
Sunderland SR1 1EA
Tel: 091 510 8933

Mon-Fri 0900-1700
NHS Open referral. Over 16 years only

MENTAL HEALTH

Community Mental Health Service
South Tyneside District Hospital
Harton Lane
South Shields NE34 0PL
Tel: 091 454 8888 ext. 2236

Mon-Fri 0900-1700
NHS Open referral. South Tyneside area

Washington MIND
31 Roche Court
Glebe
Washington NE38 7PH
Tel: 091 417 8043

Mon-Fri 1000-1600, Drop-in Mon/Tues/Thurs 1000-1500
VOL Open referral

OTHER

Women's Health in South Tyneside
St. Hilda's Youth Centre
Coronation Street
South Shields NE33 1AZ
Tel: 091 454 6959

Mon-Fri 0930-1630
VOL Open referral. Women from South Tyneside only

Warwickshire

TRANQUILLISER

COPE (Coming Over Problems Eventually)
The MIND Day Centre
Queens Road
Nuneaton
Tel: 0827 713710

Mon 1930-2115 Phone first
Telephone 0800-2000 Seven days a week
VOL Open referral

ADDICTION

Rugby Community Drug Team
The Hollies
Lower Hillmorton Road
Rugby CV21 3SS
Tel: 0788 540124/535090

Mon-Fri 0900-1700
NHS Open referral; appointment needed

MENTAL HEALTH

Mid Warwickshire MIND
3 Regent Place
Leamington Spa CV31 1EH
Tel: 0926 450745

Mon-Fri 1000-1700
Thurs 1930-2100
VOL Open referral

West Midlands

TRANQUILLISER

Slade Road Centre for Addiction
411 Slade Road
Erdington
Birmingham B23 7LA
Tel: 021 384 4855

Mon-Fri 0900-1700
NHS PUB VOL Open referral

Community Alcohol and Tranquilliser Dependency Team
45 Charlotte Road
Stirchley
Birmingham
Tel: 021 459 7884

Mon-Fri 0900-1700
NHS Open referral. South Birmingham area

Drug Care
23 Temple Street
Wolverhampton WV2 4AN
Tel: 0902 22282

Mon-Fri 0930-1700
NHS PUB Open referral.
Wolverhampton area

Coventry Tranx Support
57 Thistley Field
Coundon
Coventry CV6 2DD
Tel:0203 598126

Mon-Sun 1800-2100
VOL Open referral; telephone first

'Anchor Project' (Sandwell Community Drug Team)
c/o St. Johns Church
Price Street
Smethwick B66 3QU
Tel: 021 565 3848

Mon-Fri 1000-1700
NHS Open referral. Sandwell area

P.I.T.S. (People in Tranquilliser Situations)
Wolverhampton
Tel: 0902 787913

Mon-Fri 0930-1700; telphone advice only VOL Open referral

ADDICTION

Aquarius
84 High Street
Brierley Hill DY5 3AW
Tel: 0384 261267

Mon-Fri 0900-1700
VOL Open referral. Dudley only

West Midlands

West Midlands Regional Addiction Unit
All Saints' Hospital
Lodge Road
Winson Green
Birmingham B18 5SD
Tel: 021 523 5151 ext. 112/3

Mon-Fri 0930-1630
NHS Open referral

Turning Point Birmingham Drugline
Dale House
New Meeting Street
Birmingham B4 7SX
Tel: 021 632 6363/6364

Mon-Fri 1000-1700
(Thurs until 2000)
VOL PUB Open referral
appointment needed

Lantern House
16 Lowerhall Lane
Walsall WS1 1RL
Tel: 0922 721919

Mon-Fri 0900-1700
NHS PUB Open referral

Turning Point Dudley Drugline
Library Chambers
8 Church Street
Stourbridge DY8 1LY
Tel: 0384 375617

Weds 1200-2000, Thurs 1200-1600
NHS PUB VOL Open referral
appointment preferred

Turning Point Dudley Drugline
(also has services in Dudley and Halesowen)

MENTAL HEALTH

The Woodbourne Clinic
21 Woodbourne Road
Edgbaston B17 8BY

Tel: 021 429 4511

24 hours
PTE GP referral

Solihull MIND
14/16 Faulkner Road
Solihull B92 8SY
Tel: 021 742 4941

Mon-Fri 1000-1730, Drop-in Mon/
Weds/Thurs 1200-1630
Tues 1900-2200
VOL Open referral

OTHER

Adullam Homes Housing Association
11 Park Avenue
Hockley
Birmingham B28 5ND
Tel: 021 551 5030

Mon-Fri 0900-1700
VOL Open referral

Wiltshire

TRANQUILLISER

Tranquilliser Withdrawal/ Support Group
53 Rowden Hill House
Chippenham
Tel: 0249 659300

Mon-Fri 0900-1630
NHS Open referral. Chippenham-
Calne-Malmesbury area

ADDICTION

Alcohol and Drug Advisory Service
1 The Paragon
Wilton Road
Salisbury
Tel: 0722 412632

Mon-Fri 0900-1700
NHS Open referral; appointment
needed

Help Trowbridge Project
Bridge House
Stallard Street
Trowbridge BA14 9AE
Tel: 0225 767459

Mon-Fri 0930-1630
VOL Open referral

Druglink
174 Victoria Road
Swindon SN1 3DF
Tel: Helpline 0793 610133

Mon-Fri 0930-1630 (Weds until
2000)
NHS PUB Open referral

MENTAL HEALTH

MIND North & West Wiltshire
bridge House
Stallard Street
Trowbridge BA14 9AE
Tel: 0225 769845

Mon-Fri 1000-1600
VOL Open referral. North and West
Wiltshire

Yorkshire (North)

TRANQUILLISER

Cambridge Centre
1 Westbourne Grove
Scarborough YO11 2DJ
Tel: 0723 367475

Mon-Fri 0900-1500
NHS Open referral

ADDICTION

Airedale Community Alcohol and Drugs Team
Scalebor Park Hospital
Burley in Wharfedale
Ilkley LS29 7AJ
Tel: 0943 862031

Mon-Fri 0900-1700
NHS Open referral. Airedale District

Dragon Scheme
13 Dragon Parade (Top Floor)
Harrogate HG1 5BZ
Tel: 0423 525999

Mon-Fri 1030-1630
VOL Open referral

MENTAL HEALTH

The Retreat
107 Heslington Road
York YO1 5BN
Tel: 0904 412551

24 hours
PTE Professional referral

Harrogate & District MIND
Acorn Centre
6 Victoria Avenue
Harrogate HG1 1ED
Tel: 0423 523185

Mon/Thurs 1300-2000
Weds 1000-1700
VOL Open referral, aged over 18 years only

Yorkshire (South)

TRANQUILLISER

Shiregreen Tranx Self Help Group
c/o Mrs. L. Wilson
133 Woolley Wood Road
Shiregreen
Sheffield S5 0UF
Tel: 0742 403240

Tues 0800-2200
VOL Open referral

Rotherham Tranx Project
2 Rosehill Avenue
Rawmarsh
Rotherham
Tel: 0709 526575/549888

Mon-Fri 0900-1700, Telephone first
VOL Open referral. Rotherham area

Ecclesfield Tranx Self-Help Group
c/o Mrs. D. Radley
22 Strutt Road
Pitsmoor
Sheffield S3 9AG
Tel: 0742 758375

Mon-Fri 1700-2200
VOL Open referral

MIND in Barnsley
Dove House
156 Sheffield Road
Barnsley S70 1JH
Tel: 0226 288038

Fri 1300-1500 Group
VOL Open referral

Doncaster MIND
16 Copley Road
Doncaster DN1 2PF
Tel: 0302 322006

Mon-Fri 0900-1700
VOL Open referral

ADDICTION

Rotherham Community Drug Team
Medway House
3a Chatham Street
Rotherham SG5 1DP
Tel: 0709 382733

Mon-Fri 1000-1600
NHS PUB Open referral. Rotherham area

Rockingham Drug Project
117 Rockingham Street
Sheffield S1 4EB
Tel: 0742 580033

Mon-Fri 0930-1700
NHS PUB Open referral

Yorkshire (South)

MENTAL HEALTH

Department of Clinical Psychology
Psychology Department
11/12 Keresforth Close
Off Broadway
Barnsley S70 6RS
Tel: 0226 730000

Mon-Fri 0900-1700
NHS Open referral; appointment
needed. Barnsley area

Sheffield MIND
Lawton Tonge House
57 Wostenholm Road
Sheffield S7 1LE
Tel: 0742 584489

Mon-Fri 1000-1500
VOL Open referral

Yorkshire (West)

TRANQUILLISER

Keighley Well Women's Centre
Central Hall
Alice Street
Keighley
Tel: 0535 681316

Mon/Tues/Fri 0930-1500
Tranxline Tues 1000-1300
VOL Open referral. Women only

TASPS
Ossett Health Centre
New Street
Ossett
Tel: 0924 262285

Mon-Thurs 0800-2100
VOL Open referral

Keighley Senior Health Awareness Project
Social Centre for the Blind
31 Scott Street
Keighley
Tel:0535 604119

Mon 0900-1600, Thurs 0900-1230
24 hour telephone support
VOL Open referral. People over 50
in Keighley area

Womans Tranquillisers Support Group
5 Russell Avenue
Queensbury
Bradford

Meets second Thursday of each
month at 2015-2200
VOL Open referral

Bridge Project
Equity Chambers
40 Piccadilly
Bradford BD1 3NN
Tel: 0274 723863

Mon-Fri 1000-1630
NHS PUB Open referral

Unit 51
1st Floor, Field House
15 Wellington Road
Dewsbury
Tel: 0924 457038

Mon-Weds, Fri 0930-1730
Thurs 1330-1730,
VOL Open referral, appointment
preferred

ADDICTION

Project 6
Airedale Voluntary Drug and Alcohol Agency
6 Temple Street
Keighley BD21 2AD
Tel: 0535 610180

Mon-Fri 0900-1600
VOL Open referral

Pontefract and District Drug and Solvent Helpline (DASHLINE)
Southmoor House
Southmoor Road
Hemsworth
Pontefract WF9 4SQ
Tel: 0977 290999

24 hours
VOL NHS Open referral

Unit 51
24 Westgate
Huddersfield HD1 1NU
Tel: 0484 510826

Mon/Tues/Thurs 0930-1730
Weds 1330-2100, Fri 0930-1700
NHS VOL Open referral;
appoinment needed. Kirklees only

Airedale Community Alcohol and Drugs Team
Scalebor Park Hospital
Moor Lane
Burley in Wharfedale
Ilkley LS29 7AJ
Tel: 0943 862031

Mon-Fri 0900-1700
NHS Open referral. Airedale
district

Alcohol and Other Drug Resources Team
c/o Social Work Department
Scalebor Park Hospital
Moor Lane
Burley in Wharfedale
Ilkley LS29 7AJ
Tel: 0943 862031 ext. 2224/5

Mon-Fri 0900-1700
NHS PUB Open referral;
appointment preferred. Bradford only

Leeds Addiction Unit
19 Springfield Mount
Leeds LS2 9NG
Tel: 0532 316920 Reception,
appointments
Tel: 0532 316940 Information/
telephone counselling

Mon-Tues, Thurs-Fri 0900-1700,
Weds 0900-1300
NHS Open referral. Leeds area

Yorkshire (West) *continued*

Calderdale Community Drugs Project
Marlborough House
Crossley Street
Halifax HX1 1UG
Tel: 0422 361111

Mon-Fri 0900-1700
NHS PUB Open referral

MENTAL HEALTH

Ingrow Centre for Community Mental Health
200 South Street
Keighley BD21 1BB
Tel: 0535 665941

Mon-Fri 0900-1700
NHS PUB Professional referral.
Keighley area

OTHER

Wakefield Well Woman Centre
21 King Street
Wakefield
Tel: 0924 295370

Mon 1700-2000, Fri 1000-1300
VOL Open referral. Women only

Calderdale Well Women Centre
Harrison House
10 Harrison Road
Halifax HX1 2AF
Tel: 0422 360397

Mon/Tues 1000-1300, Weds 1730-1930, Thurs 1200-1500
Sat 1000-1200
VOL Women only

SCOTLAND
Central

TRANQUILLISER

Stirling and District MIND
4 Albert Place
Stirling
Tel: 0786 51203

Mon-Fri 0900-1100
Drop-in Mon 1000-1400
Tues 1300-1600, Fri 1300-1600
VOL Open referral

Falkirk District Association for Mental Health
Victoria Centre
102 Thornhill Road
Falkirk FK2 7AE
Tel: 0324 29955

Mon-Fri 0900-1700
VOL Open referral

Princes Street Day Hospital
5 Princes Street
Stirling
Tel: 0786 74230

Mon-Fri 0900-1700
NHS Open referral

ADDICTION

Falkirk District Drug Project
3/5 Chapel Lane
Falkirk FK1 5BB
Tel: 0324 612627

Mon-Fri 0900-1700
NHS Open referral

MENTAL HEALTH

Nu-Mar Mental Health Group
13 Mansfield Avenue
Sauchie
Alloa FK10 3LG
Tel: 0259 217382

Mon-Fri 0900-1700
VOL Open referral

Dumfries & Galloway

ADDICTION

Alcohol/Drugs Problem Unit
Hestan House
Crichton Royal Hospital
Dumfries DG1 4TG
Tel: 0387 41181

Mon-Fri 0830-1700
NHS Open referral. Dumfries &
Galloway only

MENTAL HEALTH

Threshold
9 Fineview Crescent
Glenluce DG8 0QJ
Tel: 05813 529

24 hours
VOL Open referral

Fife

Grampian

TRANQUILLISER

West Fife Support Group
92 Pittencrief Street
Dunfermline
Tel: 0383 732613

Mon-Thurs 1000-1600
Fri 1000-1200
PUB Open referral. West Fife

TRANQUILLISER

Aberdeen Drugs Action
8a Gaelic Lane
Aberdeen AB1 1JF
Tel: 0224 624555

Mon-Fri 1000-1630
NHS PUB Open referral. Aberdeen
area

Buchan Tranquility
13 Baylands Crescent
Peterhead
Tel: 0779 75251

Mon-Fri 0900-2100 Telephone first
VOL Open referral. Peterhead area

Highland

Dunain House Addiction Unit
Craig Dunain Hospital
Inverness
Tel: 0463 234101 ext. 2218

24 hours
NHS GP referral

Inverness Area Council on Alcohol
106 Church Street
Inverness
Tel: 0463 220995

Mon-Fri 0900-1700
NHS PUB Open referral

Lochaber Council on Alcohol
Caol Shopping Centre
Fort William PH33 7DR
Tel: 0397 702340

Mon-Fri 0900-1300/1400-1700
Mon-Weds 1900-2000
VOL NHS PUB Open referral
appointment advised

Lothian

Medica
Langlaw Road
Mayfield
Dalkeith EH22 5AU
Tel: 031 660 5821

Mon-Thurs 0900-1700
Fri 0900-1400
PUB Open referral

Thomas Moss
209 Crewe Road West
Edinburgh EH5 2PG
Tel: 031 552 7352

24 hours
PTE Open referral

The Windmill
40 Dumbryden Drive
Edinburgh EH14 2QR
Tel: 031 442 2484

Mon-Fri 1100-1700
PUB Open referral

West Edinburgh Support Team, Prescribed Drugs Project
8/4 Murrayburn Park
Wester Hailes
Edinburgh
Tel: 031 442 2465

Mon-Fri 0930-1700
PUB Open referral

Lothian

ADDICTION

Muirhouse/Pilton Drug Project
Department of Social Work
34 Muirhouse Crescent
Muirhouse
Edinburgh EH4 4QL
Tel: 031 343 1991

Mon-Thurs 0830-1640
Fri 0830-1550
PUB Open referral; appointment
needed. Muirhouse & Pilton area

Drug & Alcohol Project (West Lothian)
47 Adelaide Street
Craigshill
Livingston EH54 5HQ
Tel: 0506 30225

Mon-Fri 0930-1700
NHS Open referral; appointment
needed. Lothian region

MENTAL HEALTH

Craigentinny Health Project
Community Centre
Loaning Road
Edinburgh
Tel: 031 661 8188

Mon-Thurs 0900-1630
PUB Open referral; telephone first

OTHER

Broxburn Family Centre
1-3 Henderson Place
Broxburn
Tel: 0506 855301

Mon-Fri 1000-1630
PUB Open referral

Strathclyde

TRANQUILLISER

Trouble with Tranquillizers
5 Hawthorn Drive
Greenend
Coatbridge
Tel: 0236 40966

Mon-Fri 0900-1700
PUB Open referral; women only
Monklands area

Pollok Addiction Information and Advice Centre
The Linthargh Centre
20 Linthaugh Road
Pollok
Glasgow G53
Tel: 041 810 5200

Mon-Thurs 0900-1645
Fri 0900-1600
PUB Open referral

Inverclyde Drugline
3 Shaw Place
Greenock
Tel: 0475 888053

Mon-Fri 0900-1700
Thurs 1830-2100
PUB VOL Open referral. Inverclyde area

Renfrew Substance Abuse Resource Centre
20 Back Sneddon Street
Paisley
Tel: 041 889 1223

Mon-Thurs 0845-1645
Fri 0845-1555
PUB Open referral

Listening Ear Tranx Self Help Group
Castlemilk Health Centre
Dougrie Drive
Glasgow G45
Tel: 041 634 3434

Mon/Weds 1300-1600, telephone
counselling Mon-Fri 0900-2000 Tel:
041 631 2244
VOL Open referral

Freedom From Tranquillisers
Possilpoint
Denmark Street
Glasgow G22 5BW
Tel: 041 336 6484

Meets Fri 1300-1700, telephone
Mon-Fri 0900-1700
VOL Open referral

Strathclyde

ADDICTION

Church of Scotland 'Rainbow House'
1 Belhaven Terrace
Glasgow G12
Tel: 041 339 2691

24 hours
VOL Drug Worker/Social Worker referral

Church of Scotland Board of Social Responsibility
Ronachan House
Clachan
Tarbert
Tel: 08804 252

Mon-Fri 0900-1700
VOL Open referral; must negotiate fees with Social Work department

Information Unit on Addiction
Room 7, First Floor
McIver House
51 Cadogan Street
Glasgow G2 7QB
Tel: 041 204 3566

Mon-Thurs 0845-1645, Fri 0845-1555
PUB Open referral

Cambuslang Addiction Project
13 Main Street
Cambuslang
Tel: 041 641 7038/7048

Mon-Fri 0900-1700
PUB Open referral

Vernon Centre
35 Vernon Street
Saltcoats KA21 5HE
Tel:0294 61731

Mon/Weds 0900-1700, Tues/Thurs 0900-2100, Fri 0900-1600
PUB Open referral; appointment preferred. Saltcoats, Ardrossan, Largs, Stevenson and Garnock Valley

Drug Project
Southern General Hospital
Govan Road
Glasgow G51 4TF
Tel: 041 440 0741 ext. 6487

Mon-Fri 0900-1700
NHS PUB Open referral

Candle Addiction Advice Centre
5 South Muirhead Road
Cumbernauld G67 1AX
Tel: 0236 731378

Mon-Thurs 0930-1700 and 1900-2200, Fri 0900-1600
Helpline 0236 35539 24 hours
NHS Open referral

Strathclyde *continued*

Easterhouse Committee on Drug Abuse (ECODA)
8-12 Armisdale Road
Easterhouse
Glasgow G34
Tel: 041 773 2001

Mon-Thurs 0900-1700
Fri 0900-1600
NHS Open referral

Monkland Addiction Advisory Centre
81c Hallcraig Street
Airdrie ML6 4AN
Tel: 0236 753341

Mon-Fri 0900-2100
PUB Open referral

Calderhead Addiction Unit
Kirk Road
Shotts
Tel: 0501 23539

Mon-Fri 0900-1700
PUB Open referral

Addiction Unit
Ruchill Hospital
Bilsland Drive
Glasgow
Tel: 041 946 7120 ext. 1215/1218

Mon-Fri 0900-1900
NHS Open referral; appointment needed

Shield Centre
Social Work Department
Strathclyde Regional Council
27/29 Hill Street
Wishaw ML2 7AT
Tel: 0698 355865

Mon 0845-1645, Tues-Thurs 0845-2215, Fri 0845-1555, Sat 0900-1200
PUB Open referral

Bellshill Cross Day Centre
Strathclyde Regional Council
Social Work Department
171 Main Street
Bellshill ML4 1AH
Tel: 0698 749546

Mon-Fri 0845-1645
PUB Open referral

The Bridge Project
17 River Street
Ayr KA8 0AX
Tel: 0292 287777

Mon-Fri 0900-1700
VOL Open referral

Drugline
3 Holmston Road
Ayr
Tel:0292 610868 and 0292 262111

Mon-Fri 0900-1700
NHS PUB Open referral. South Ayrshire only

Strathclyde

Scottish Drugs Forum
5 Oswald Street
Glasgow G1 4QR
Tel: 041 221 1175

Mon-Fri 0930-1630
PUB Open referral

Alexandria Drop-in Centre
85 Bank Street
Alexandria
Tel: 0389 51343

Mon-Fri 0900-1630
Mon-Thurs 1830-2030
PUB Open referral

Townhead Centre
45 Townhead
Irvine KA12 0BH
Tel: 0294 75631/73895

Mon-Thurs 0845-1645
Fri 0845-1555
PUB Open referral

Gorbals Detached Drug Project
c/o 44 South Portland Street
Glasgow G5
Tel: 041 429 3411

Mon-Fri 0900-1700
NHS PUB Open referral

MENTAL HEALTH

Stepping Stones
Alexander Resource Centre
83 Blair Road
Coatbridge
Tel: 0236 22544 and 0236 769344
ext. 375

Meets 2nd and 4th Weds 1900-2100
Telephone Mon-Fri 0900-1700
PUB Open referral

OTHER

Ballantay Well Woman
9 Ballantay Quad
Castlemilk
Glasgow G45 00P
Tel: 041 631 1198

Weds 0900-1530
NHS Open referral. Women only

Tayside

TRANQUILLISER

Dundee Y.M.C.A. Drug & AIDS Project
76 Bell Street
Dundee DD1 1HF
Tel: 0382 200532

Mon-Fri 0900-1700
VOL Open referral. Tayside area

ADDICTION

Drug Problems Centre
Constitution House
55 Constitution Road
Dundee DD1 1LA
Tel: 0382 25083

Mon/Weds/Thurs/Fri 0900-1200
Tues 1100-1200, 1300-1600
Weds/Fri 1300-1600
NHS Open referral. Tayside area

MENTAL HEALTH

Perth MIND
6 Milne Street
Perth PH1 5QL
Tel: 0738 39657

Mon-Fri 0900-1300, 1400-1600
VOL Open referral. Perth area

Dundee MIND
Kandahar House Centre
71 Meadowside
Dundee DD1 1EN
Tel: 0382 27288

Mon-Fri 0900-1600
VOL Open referral

Western Isles

ADDICTION

Skye and Lochalsh Council on Alcohol
Highland Regional Council
Offices
Dunvegan Road
Portree
Isle of Skye IV51 9HD
Tel: 0478 2633

Mon-Fri 0900-1700
NHS PUB Open referral
appointment needed

WALES
Clwyd

ADDICTION

Drug Dependency Unit, Gwydyr Ward
North Wales Hospital
Denbigh LL16 5SS
Tel: 0745 812871 ext. 271

24 hours
NHS Referral from Clwyd &
Gwynedd Drug Advisory Service

Clwyd Health Authority Drugs Service (Co-ordinator's office)
Preswylfa
Hendy Road
Mold CH7 1PZ
Tel: 0352 700227

Mon-Fri 0900-1700
NHS Open referral; appointment
advisable. Clwyd area

Clwyd Health Authority Drugs Service
21b Chester Road West
Shotton
Deeside
Tel: 0244 831798

Mon-Fri 0900-1700
NHS Open referral; appointment
advisable. Clwyd area

Clwyd Health Authority Drugs Service
2 Market Street
Rhyl
Tel: 0745 338868

Mon-Fri 0900-1700
NHS Open referral; appointment
advisable. Clwyd area

Clwyd Health Authority Drugs Service
Bod Alaw
Rivieres Avenue
Colwyn Bay
Tel: 0492 534435

MENTAL HEALTH

Vale of Clwyd MIND Association
34 Elwy Street
Rhyl
Tel: 0745 336787

Mon-Fri 1000-1600
VOL Open referral Vale of Clwyd
area

Dyfed

ADDICTION

Carmarthen Drugs Project
The Lodge
1 Penlan
Carmarthen
Tel: 0267 222107

Mon-Thurs 1000-1600
Fri 1400-1600
NHS Open referral
Carmarthen/Dinefwr area

Rhoserchan Project
Capel Seion
Aberystwyth SY23 4ED
Tel: 0970 611127

Mon-Fri 0900-1700
VOL Open referral

Llanelli Drugs Project
4a Cowell Street
Llanelli
Tel: 0554 756273

Mon-Thurs 1000-1600
Fri 1400-1600
NHS Open referral. Llanelli area

MENTAL HEALTH

Department of Clinical Psychology
St. David's Hospital
Carmarthen SA31 3HB
Tel: 0267 237481 ext. 4581

Mon-Thurs 0900-1700
Fri 0900-1630
NHS Open referral, but GP must be told. Carmarthen area

Gwent

TRANQUILLISER

Tranquilliser Self Help Group
Kensington Court Day Centre
Oaklands Road
Maindy
Newport NP9 8GQ
Tel: 0633 290330

Drop-in Mon 1900-2030
VOL Open referral

ADDICTION

Gwent Drug Project
139 Lower Dock Street
Newport NP9 1EE
Tel: 0633 216777

Tues-Thurs 0900-1700
Fri 0900-1630
NHS Open referral; appointment
preferred

MENTAL HEALTH

Maindiff Court Hospital
Ross Road
Abergavenny NP7 8NF
Tel: 0873 852343

24 hours
NHS Professional referral.
Pontypool area

Gwynedd

TRANQUILLISER

Bangor MIND
9 Abbey Road
Bangor LL57 2EA
Tel: 0248 354888

Mon-Fri 0900-1700
VOL Open referral

ADDICTION

Holyhead Drug Care Group
Tel: 0407 760817

24 hours
VOL Open referral. All of Anglesey

Mid Glamorgan

TRANQUILLISER

Social Services Department
55 Cemetery Road
Trecynon
Aberdare
Tel: 0685 875481

Mon-Fri 0900-1700
PUB Open referral

Treorchy Trust Group
55 High Street
Treorchy CF42 6NR
Tel: 0443 773864

Mon-Fri 0900-1700, telephone first
VOL Open referral

GUTS (Giving Up Tranquillisers)
12 Heol Dewi
Hengoed
Tel: 0443 813167

Mon-Fri 1000-1630
VOL Open referral; appointment needed. Rhymney Valley area

ADDICTION

Taff Ely Drug Support Group
Cottage 4
Garth Olwg
Church Village
Pontypridd CF38 1BT
Tel: 0443 203344

Mon-Fri 0900-1300/1800-2100
VOL Open referral

Mid Glamorgan Community Drug Team
Llwyn yr Eos Clinic
Main Road
Church Village
Pontypridd CF38 1RN
Tel: 0443 217026

Mon-Thurs 0900-1700
Fri 0900-1630
NHS Professional referral appointment needed

Mid Glamorgan

MENTAL HEALTH

Fresh Start
Cottage 4
Garth Olwg
Church Village
Pontypridd CF38 1BT
Tel: 0443 203344

Mon-Fri 0900-1300/1800-2100
VOL Open referral

OTHER

Rhondda Womens Aid
P.O. Box 1
Ton Pentre
Rhondda
Tel: 0443 431138

Mon-Fri 0900-1700
PUB Open referral. Women only

South Glamorgan

TRANQUILLISER

Barry Tranx
234 Holton Road
Barry
Tel: 0446 750411

Mon-Fri 1000-1700
VOL Open referral

ADDICTION

South Wales Association for the Prevention of Addiction Ltd.
1 Neville Street
Cardiff CF1 8LP
Tel: 0222 383313

24 hours
VOL Open referral

LIBRA (Wales)
Tegfan Day Hospital
Whitchurch Hospital
Cardiff
Tel: 0222 693191 ext. 6593

Meets Fri 1400-1600 at Barnardo's
Shop, Caerau Lane, Ely Cardiff
VOL Open referral

South Glamorgan Community Drug Team
46 Cowbridge Road East
Cardiff CF1 9DU
Tel: 0222 395877

Mon-Fri 0900-1700
NHS Open referral; appointment
needed. South Glamorgan

West Glamorgan

ADDICTION

West Glamorgan Council on Alcohol and Drug Abuse
Alcohol and Drugs Advice
Centre
75 Uplands Crescent
Uplands
Swansea SA2 0EX
Tel: 0742 472519

Mon-Fri 0900-1700
NHS Open referral

Swansea Drugs Project (SAND)
8 Calvert Terrace
Uplands
Swansea SA1 6AR
Tel: 0792 472002

Mon-Wed 1000-1600
Fri 1000-1600, Sat 1100-1300
VOL NHS Open referral

MENTAL HEALTH

Neath MIND
41 Milland Road
Neath
Tel: 0639 643510

Sun-Fri 1030-1730
24 hour helpline 0639 750837
VOL Open referral

Index by Town

New Services Notification

If you provide or know of a service not included in this Directory, please let us know. It will be incorporated, if appropriate, into the next edition and will be of use in our referral activities. Thank you.

- -

BLOCK CAPITALS OR TYPE PLEASE

1 Name of Service _____

2 Address and Telephone _____

_____

3 Description of Service (What it does, and for whom) _____

_____

_____

_____

4 When Open/available _____

5 Any charge made? (amount) _____

Please return to: MIND
                 22 Harley Street
                 LONDON W1N 2ED